Frontispiece.

Mrs. MARGERY TWO-SHOES

Governess of

A. B. C. College.

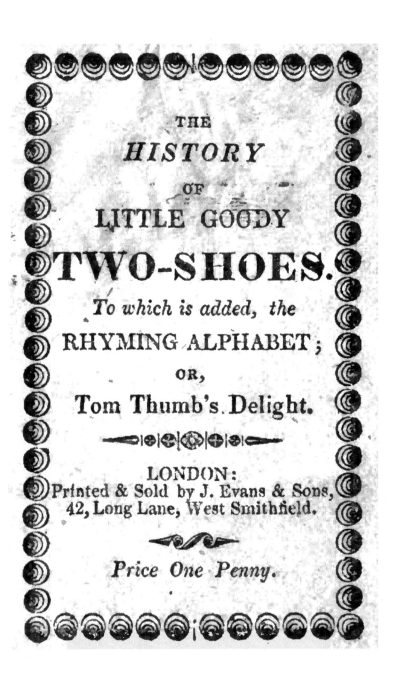

THE

HISTORY

OF

LITTLE GOODY

TWO-SHOES.

To which is added, the

RHYMING ALPHABET;

OR,

Tom Thumb's Delight.

LONDON:

Printed & Sold by J. Evans & Sons,
42, Long Lane, West Smithfield.

Price One Penny.

History of Little
Goody Two-Shoes.

ALL the world must allow
that Two-Shoes was not her real
name: No, her father's name was
Meanwell, and he was for many
years a considerable farmer in the
parish where Margery was born;
but by the misfortunes he met
with in business, and the wick-
ed persecutions of Sir Timothy
Gripe, and an overgrown farmer, called Graspall, he was effec-
tually ruined. A little time put

a period to his existence, and his two children, Tommy and Margery, were left orphans.

It would have excited your pity and done your heart good to have seen how fond these two little ones were of one another,

and how, hand in hand, they trotted about; Tommy had two shoes, but Margery had but one;

they had nothing, poor things!
to support them, but what they
picked from the hedges, or got
from the poor people, and they
lay every night in a barn. Their
relations took no notice of them;
no, they were rich, and ashamed
to own such poor little children.
However, a gentleman, whose
name was Kindheart, took Tommy and made him a sailor.

Mr. Smith, a worthy clergy-man, sent for a shoemaker, and ordered Madge a pair of new ones. As soon as she received them, and had put them on, she was mightily pleased with them, and ran to Mrs. Smith, and strok-ing down her apron, cried out, "Two Shoes, Mame, see Two Shoes!" and so she behaved to every one she met, and by that means obtained the name of Goody Two Shoes.

Little Margery saw how wise and good Mr. Smith was, and concluded that this was owing to his great learning; she there-fore wanted above all other things to learn to read. For this purpose she used to meet the little boys and girls as they came from school, borrow their books, and read them till they returned. By this means she got more learning than any of her playmates, and then laid the following scheme for instructing those who were more ignorant than herself. She found that only the following letters are required to spell all the words in the world; but as some of these letters are large and some small, she with a knife cut out of several pieces of wood ten sets of each of these:

a b c d e f g h i j k l m n o p
q r s t u v w x y z

And six sets of these :

A B C D E F G H I J K L M
N O P Q R S T U V W X Y Z

And having got an old spelling
book, she made her companions
set up all the words they wanted
to spell, and after that she taught
them to compose sentences.—
You know what a sentence is,
my dear, I will be good, is a
sentence, and is made up, as
you see, of several words.

The usual manner of spelling
or carrying on the game, as they
call it, was this: Suppose the
word to be spelt was plum-pud-
ding, the children were placed
in a circle, and the first brought
the letter P, next l, the next u,

the next m, and so on till the whole was spelt; and if any one brought a wrong letter, he was to pay a fine or play no more. This was at their play. And every morning she used to go round to

teach the children with these rattle traps. I once went her rounds with her, and was highly diverted, as you may be, if you read on.

It was about seven o'clock in the morning when we set out on this important business, and the first house we came to was Farmer Wilson's. Here we stopped, and Margery went up to the door, tap, tap. "Who's there?" "Only little Goody Two-Shoes," answered Margery,— "come to teach Billy." "Oh! little Goody," says Mrs. Wilson with pleasure in her face, "I am glad to see you: Billy wants you sadly, for he has learned all his lesson." Then out came the little boy: "How do,—Doody Two Shoes," says he, not able to

speak plain. Yet this little boy
had learned all his letters; for
she threw down the alphabet
mixed together thus:

d b f h k m o q s u v w y x a
g z e c i l n p r t x j

and he picked them all up, called
them by their right names, and
put them all in order thus:

a b c d e f g h i j k l m n o
p q r s t u v w x y z

She then threw down the alphabet of capital letters in the
manner you here see them:

B D F H K M O Q S U W Y Z
A C E G I L N P R X T V J

and he picked them all up, and
having told their names, placed
them thus;

A B C D E F G H I J K L M
N O P Q R S T U V W X Y Z

Now, pray little reader, take
this bodkin, and see if you can
point out the letters from these
mixed alphabets, and tell how
they should be placed as well as
the little boy Billy.

The next place we came to was
Farmer Simpson's. Bow wow-
wow, says the dog at the house

door: "Sirrah!" says his mistress,
why do you bark at little Two
Shoes? Come in, Madge; here is
Sally wants you sadly, she has
learned all her lesson. Then out
came the little one. "So Madge!"
said she; "So Sally!" answered
the other, have you learned your
lesson?" "Yes, that's what I have,"
replied the little one in the coun-
try manner; and immediately ta-
king the letters, she set up these
syllables:

ba be bi bo bu   ca ce ci co cu
da de di do du   fa fe fi fo fu

and gave them their exact sounds
as she composed them; after this,
she set up the following -

This is the cock that crow'd in the morn,
That wak'd the Priest all shaven and shorn.

As we were returning home
we saw a gentleman who was very ill, sitting under a shady tree
at the corner of his rookery. Tho'
ill, he began to joke with little
Margery, and said, laughing, "So
Goody Two Shoes, they tell me
you are a cunning little baggage;
pray can you tell me what I shall
do to get well?" "Yes, Sir," says

she, go to bed when your rooks
do; you see they are going to
rest already; do you so likewise,
and get up with them in the
morning; earn as they do, every
day, what you eat, and you will
get health and keep it.—What
should induce rooks to frequent
gentlemen's houses only, but to
tell them how to lead a prudent
life? They never build over cot-
tages or farm-houses, because
they see that these people know
how to live without their admo-
nition.

Thus health and wit you may improve,
Taught by the tenants of the grove.

The gentleman laughing, gave
Margery sixpence, and told her
she was a sensible hussey.

Goody Two-Shoes continued to go her rounds for some time; at length a Tutoress was wanted in A B C College, and she was elected without opposition. Here her wisdom and goodness was obvious to every body, and her fame spread far and wide.

Having an uncommon understanding, the neighbours courted her company, and she frequently favoured them with it. While at Mr. Grove's, which was in the heart of the village, she not only taught the children in the day-time, but the farmer's servants, and all the neighbours to read and write in the evening; and it was the common practice

before they went away, to make
them all go to prayers and sing
psalms. By these means the
people grew extremely regular,
his servants were always at home,
instead of being at the ale-house
they strictly attended church,
and he had more work done than
ever.

This gave not only Mr. Grove,
but all the neighbours, an high
opinion of her sense and prudent
behaviour, and she was so much
esteemed that most of the differ-
ences in the parish were left to
her decision; even when children fell out at play, and could
not settle it among themselves,
they must needs refer it to Mrs.

Margery for the satisfaction of
all parties; and if any man and
wife quarrelled, (which some-
times happened in that part of
the kingdom) both parties cer-
tainly came to her for advice.

Every body knows that Martha Wilson was a very passion-
ate scolding jade, and that John
her husband, was a surly, ill-

tempered fellow; these were once brought by the neighbours, for Margery to talk with, when they fairly quarrelled before her face, and were going to blows, but she stepping between them, said to the husband, John, says she, you are a man, and you ought to know your duty better than to fly in a passion at every word that is said amiss by your wife; and you Martha, says she, ought to have more sense than to say any thing to aggravate your husband's resentment.—— These frequent quarrels arise from the indulgence of your very violent passions: for I know you both love one another, notwith-

standing all that has passed between you: now pray tell me
John, and tell me Martha, when
you have had a quarrel over
night, are you not both sorry
for it the next day? They both
declared that they were. Why
then, says she, I will tell you
how to prevent it in future, if
you will promise to take my advice: they both promised they
would. You know, says she,
that a small spark will set fire
to tinder, and that tinder pro-
perly placed will fire an house;
an angry word is with you as
that spark, for you are both as
touchy as tinder, and often make
your house too hot to hold you.

To prevent this in future, and to live happily, you must solemnly agree, that if one speak an angry word the other will not answer till he or she has distinctly called over all the letters in the alphabet, and that the other shall not reply till he or she has told twenty; by these means your passion will be stifled, and reason will have time to take the rule.

This is the best recipe ever given for a married couple to live in peace: though John and his wife frequently attempted to quarrel afterwards, they could never get their passions to any considerable height, for there was something so uncommonly droll in thus carrying on the dispute, that before they got to the end of the argument, they saw the absurdity of it, laughed, kissed, and were friends.

Just as Mrs. Margaret had settled the difference between John and his wife, the children who had been sent out to play while that business was transacting, returned, some in tears, and others very disconsolate, for the loss of a little dormouse they were fond of, and which was just dead.

Mrs. Margery who had the art of moralizing and drawing instruction from every accident in life, took this opportunity of reading them a lecture on the uncertainty of life, and the necessity of being always prepared for death.

After this she permitted the children to bury the little dormouse, and desired one of the little boys to write the following

Epitaph on a Dormouse.

In paper case,
Hard by this place,
Dead a poor dormouse lies;
And soon or late,
Summon'd by fate,
Each prince, each monarch dies.

Ye sons of verse,
While I rehearse,
Attend instructive rhyme:
No sins had Dor
To answer for:
Repent of yours in time.

End of Goody Two-Shoes.

Rhyming Alphabet;

Or, Tom Thumb's Delight.

A Was an Angler,
And he caught a Fish;

B Was a Brazier,
And he made a Dish.

C Was a Cook,
And he fill'd it with Broth;

D Was a Driver,
Quite sullen in Sloth.

E Was an Eater,
And gorg'd all Day long;

F Was a Fiddler,
And sung a good song.

G Was a Giant,
Both surly and stout;

H Was a Huntsman,
And rov'd all about.

I Was an Innkeeper,
Who sold us good Ale;

K Was a King,
That would often regale.

L Was a Liar,
By all men abhorr'd;

M Was a Merchant,
As rich as a Lord.

N Was a Noodle,
And fond of the Bow;

O Was an Oaf,
Who follow'd the Plough.

P Was a Ploughman,
That work'd all the day;

Q Was a Queen,
That went to the Play.

R Run a Race by himself,
And was beat;

S Was a Slut,
And spoil'd all the Meat.

T Was a Traitor,
And deserved to swing:

V Vow'd him Vengeance,
And told it the King.

W Was a Warrior,
Stout, active, and bold;

X Was Xantippe,
That arrant old Scold.

Y Was a Youth,
A pretty good Lad;

Z Was a Zany,
Altogether quite bad.

FINIS.

Marsden, Printer, Chelmsford.

PKXX

10⁰¹

Printed in the USA
CPSIA information can be obtained
at www.ICGtesting.com
LVHW022129200923
758456LV00079B/327